A Publication of the
National Wildfire Coordinating Group

Sponsored by
United States Department of Agriculture

United States Department of the Interior

National Association of State Foresters

Recreation Area Fire Prevention

PMS 457
NFES 2601

March 1999

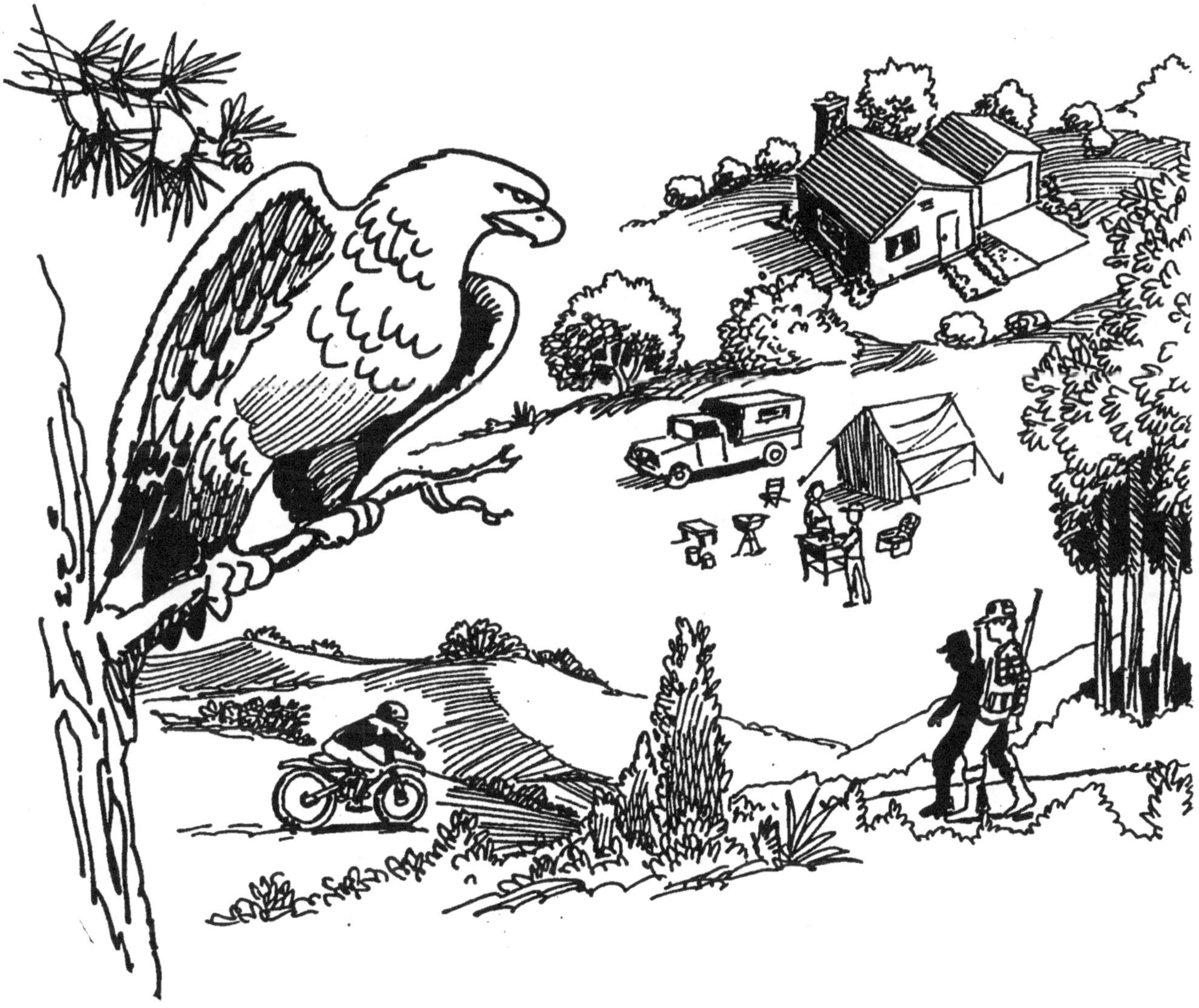

Recreation Area
Fire Prevention

Sponsored for NWCG publication bt the Fire Prevention Working Team, March 1999

Additional copies of this publication may be ordered from:
National Interagency Fire Center,
ATTN: Great Basin Cache Supply Office,
3833 S. Development Ave., Boise Id 83705.
Order NFES #2601

Preface

This Wildfire Prevention Guide is a project of the National Wildfire Coordinating Group. This guide is one in a series designed to provide information and guidance for personnel who have interests and/or responsibilities in fire prevention.

Each guide in the series addresses an individual component of a fire prevention program. In addition to providing insight and useful information, each guide suggests implementation strategies and examples for utilizing this information.

Each Wildfire Prevention Guide has been developed by Fire Prevention Specialists and subject matter experts in the appropriate area. The goal of this series is to improve and enhance wildfire prevention programs and to facilitate the achievement of NWCG program goals.

NWCG Wildfire Prevention Guide development:

- Conducting School Programs (1996)
- Event Management (1996)
- Wildfire Prevention Marketing (1996)
- Wildfire Prevention and the Media (1998)
- Wildfire Prevention Strategies (1998)
- Effective Wildfire Prevention Patrol (1998)
- Recreation Area Fire Prevention (1999)
- Fire Communication and Education (1999)
- Fire Education Exhibits and Displays (1999)
- Industrial Operations Fire Prevention Guide (1999)

Contents

Appendix

Recreation Area Fire Evaluation Report

*I*ntroduction   *1.0*

Recreation can be defined as the "use of leisure time to freely engage in activities in a variety of settings which provide personal satisfaction and enjoyment and contribute to the 'renewal' and 'refreshment' of one's body, mind and spirit."

Agency actions taken to manage recreation activities include:

- Aiding in the visitor's use and enjoyment of the Public Lands;
- Meeting agency recreation objectives for the protection and/or enhancement of recreation resources;
- Providing certain types of recreation opportunities.

Actions that provide a direct service to visitors include providing information, maps, signs, supervising use and patrolling.

Areas of high human use will increase the potential for increased fire occurrence. To provide adequate fire protection, planning for public and agency fire safety and loss prevention should begin at the earliest possible date. This guide will provide information on developing fire safe recreation areas.

Notes

*R*ecreation Area Developments   *2.0*

Recreation areas are designed for public enjoyment. The result is an increase in use which results in an increased potential for wildfire resulting in damage to natural resources, loss of improvements and risk to life. This section considers the following to assist in development of a fire safe recreation area:

    2.1   Developed Recreation Sites

    2.2   Dispersed/Undeveloped Recreation Areas

    2.3   Wilderness/Back Country

    2.4   Other Recreational Areas

*D*eveloped Recreation Sites

2.1

A recreation site is developed primarily to accommodate specific use activities or groupings of activities such as camping, picnicking, boating, swimming, day use, etc. These sites include permanent facilities such as roads, trails, toilets and other facilities needed to accommodate recreation use over the long term and require continuing commitment and regular maintenance.

I. RECREATION ACTIVITIES/USES ASSOCIATED WITH DEVELOPED SITES

- ■ Camping
- ■ Fishing
- ☐ Trapping
- ☐ Hunting
- ■ Boating
- ☐ Hiking
- ☐ Backpacking
- ☐ Horseback
- ■ Water Sports (Rivers, Lakes, etc.)
- ☐ Recreational Gold Panning
- ■ Off Highway Vehicle - Motorized
- ■ Off Highway Vehicle - Non-Motorized (Mountain Bikes, etc.)
- ■ Hang Gliding (Aerial Activities)
- ■ Rock Climbing
- ■ Resorts
- ■ Hobby Collecting (Rock Hounding)
- ■ Cultural Activities

☐ Caving

■ Party Areas

■ Special Events

■ Educational Programs

II. POTENTIAL IGNITION RISKS AT DEVELOPED RECREATION SITES

☐ Wildland/Urban Interface

☐ Wildland/Urban Intermix

☐ Maintenance Projects

☐ Construction Projects

☐ Power Lines/Substations

☐ Agriculture/Ranching

☐ Mining

☐ Railroads

☐ Power Equipment

■ Water Based Recreation

■ Campgrounds

■ Transportation Corridors

■ Fireworks

☐ Shooting Areas

■ Children with Matches

■ Incendiary

☐ Debris Burn

☐ Slash Burn

☐ Timber Operations

■ OHV

■ Hunters

■ Fishermen

☐ Party Areas

☐ Trails/Hikers

■ Camps/Resorts

☐ Business

☐ Schools

☐ Dumps

☐ Dispersed Recreation

☐ Fuelwood/Equipment

☐ Communication Sites

■ Cultural Activities

☐ Drug Labs/Cultivation

III. POTENTIAL FIRE CAUSES AT DEVELOPED RECREATION SITES

■ Cooking/Warming Fire

■ Smoking

☐ Trash Burning

☐ Burning Vehicle

■ Exhaust/Catalytic Converter

☐ Logging Line

☐ Brakeshoe

☐ Burning Dump

☐ Field Burning

☐ Land Cleaning

☐ Slash Burning

☐ Right-of-Way/Ditch Burning

☐ Resource Management Burn

☐ Grudge Fires

- ■ Intentional (Arson, Employment, Pyromania, etc.)
- ☐ Blasting
- ☐ Burning Building
- ■ Playing with Matches
- ☐ House/Stove Spark
- ☐ Power Line/Transformer
- ■ Fireworks
- ☐ Welding
- ☐ Railroad
- ■ Shooting

Dispersed / Undeveloped Recreation Areas

2.2

Dispersed/undeveloped Recreation Areas are used for activities such as camping, day use, etc., but not specifically developed for that purpose. Facilities are usually temporary in nature, designed to minimize resource damage and provided for short-term use. Although little or no investment may have been made at these areas, they are periodically monitored and maintained.

I. RECREATION ACTIVITIES/USES ASSOCIATED WITH DISPERSED/UNDEVELOPED AREAS

- Camping
- Fishing
- Trapping
- Hunting
- Boating
- Hiking
- Backpacking
- Horseback
- Water Sports (Rivers, Lakes, etc.)
- Recreational Gold Panning
- Off Highway Vehicle - Motorized
- Off Highway Vehicle - Non-Motorized (Mountain Bikes, etc.)
- Hang Gliding (Aerial Activities)
- Rock Climbing
- ☐ Resorts
- Hobby Collecting (Rock Hounding)

- Cultural Activities
- Caving
- Party Areas
- Special Events
- Educational Programs

II. POTENTIAL IGNITION RISKS IN DISPERSED/ UNDEVELOPED AREAS

- ☐ Wildland/Urban Interface
- ☐ Wildland/Urban Intermix
- ■ Maintenance Projects
- ■ Construction Projects
- ☐ Power Lines/Substations
- ☐ Agriculture/Ranching
- ■ Mining
- ☐ Railroads
- ■ Power Equipment
- ■ Water Based Recreation
- ■ Campgrounds
- ■ Transportation Corridors
- ■ Fireworks
- ■ Shooting Areas
- ■ Children with Matches
- ■ Incendiary
- ☐ Debris Burn
- ☐ Slash Burn
- ☐ Timber Operations
- ■ OHV
- ■ Hunters

- ■ Fishermen
- ■ Party Areas
- ■ Trails/Hikers
- ☐ Camps/Resorts
- ☐ Business
- ☐ Schools
- ☐ Dumps
- ■ Dispersed Recreation
- ☐ Fuelwood/Equipment
- ☐ Communication Sites
- ■ Cultural Activities
- ☐ Drug Labs/Cultivation

III. POTENTIAL FIRE CAUSES IN DISPERSED/ UNDEVELOPED RECREATION AREAS

- ■ Cooking/Warming Fire
- ■ Smoking
- ☐ Trash Burning
- ☐ Burning Vehicle
- ■ Exhaust/Catalytic Converter
- ☐ Logging Line
- ☐ Brakeshoe
- ☐ Burning Dump
- ☐ Field Burning
- ☐ Land Cleaning
- ☐ Slash Burning
- ☐ Right-of-Way/Ditch Burning
- ☐ Resource Management Burn

- ☐ Grudge Fires
- ■ Intentional (Arson, Employment, Pyromania, etc.)
- ☐ Blasting
- ☐ Burning Building
- ■ Playing with Matches
- ☐ House/Stove Spark
- ☐ Power Line/Transformer
- ■ Fireworks
- ☐ Welding
- ☐ Railroad
- ■ Shooting

Wilderness/Back Country

Wilderness or back country, in contrast with those areas where human activity dominates the landscape, is recognized as an area where the earth and its community of life are largely untrammeled by humans, where humans are visitors who do not remain for extended periods of time. An area of wilderness is further defined to mean in this influence, without permanent improvements or harm habitation, which is protected and managed so as to preserve its natural conditions and which:

- Greatly appears to have been affected primarily by the forces of nature with the imprint of human work substantially unnoticeable.

- Has outstanding opportunities for solitude or a primitive and unconfined type of recreation.

- Is of sufficient size as to make predictable its preservation and use in an unimproved condition.

- May contain ecological, geological or other features of scientific, educational or historical value.

I. RECREATION ACTIVITIES/USES ASSOCIATED WITH WILDERNESS AND BACK COUNTRY AREAS

- Camping
- Fishing
- Trapping
- Hunting
- Boating
- Hiking

- ■ Backpacking
- ■ Horseback
- ■ Water Sports (Rivers, Lakes, etc.)
- ■ Recreational Gold Panning
- ☐ Off Highway Vehicle - Motorized
- ■ Off Highway Vehicle - Non-Motorized (Mountain Bikes, etc.)
- ■ Hang Gliding (Aerial Activities)
- ■ Rock Climbing
- ☐ Resorts
- ■ Hobby Collecting (Rock Hounding)
- ■ Cultural Activities
- ■ Caving
- ☐ Party Areas
- ☐ Special Events
- ■ Educational Programs

II. POTENTIAL IGNITION RISKS IN WILDERNESS AND BACK COUNTRY AREAS

- ☐ Wildland/Urban Interface
- ☐ Wildland/Urban Intermix
- ■ Maintenance Projects
- ☐ Construction Projects
- ☐ Power Lines/Substations
- ☐ Agriculture/Ranching
- ■ Mining
- ☐ Railroads
- ☐ Power Equipment
- ■ Water Based Recreation

- ☐ Campgrounds
- ☐ Transportation Corridors
- ■ Fireworks
- ■ Shooting Areas
- ■ Children with Matches
- ■ Incendiary
- ☐ Debris Burn
- ☐ Slash Burn
- ☐ Timber Operations
- ☐ OHV
- ■ Hunters
- ■ Fishermen
- ☐ Party Areas
- ■ Trails/Hikers
- ☐ Camps/Resorts
- ☐ Business
- ☐ Schools
- ☐ Dumps
- ■ Dispersed Recreation
- ☐ Fuelwood/Equipment
- ☐ Communication Sites
- ■ Cultural Activities
- ☐ Drug Labs/Cultivation

III. POTENTIAL FIRE CAUSES IN WILDERNESS AND BACK COUNTRY AREAS

- ■ Cooking/Warming Fire
- ■ Smoking

- ☐ Trash Burning
- ☐ Burning Vehicle
- ☐ Exhaust/Catalytic Converter
- ☐ Logging Line
- ☐ Brakeshoe
- ☐ Burning Dump
- ☐ Field Burning
- ☐ Land Cleaning
- ☐ Slash Burning
- ☐ Right-of-Way/Ditch Burning
- ☐ Resource Management Burn
- ☐ Grudge Fires
- ■ Intentional (Arson, Employment, Pyromania, etc.)
- ☐ Blasting
- ☐ Burning Building
- ■ Playing with Matches
- ☐ House/Stove Spark
- ☐ Power Line/Transformer
- ■ Fireworks
- ☐ Welding
- ☐ Railroad
- ■ Shooting

*O*ther Recreational Areas 2.4

SCENIC ROADWAYS

These are determined by scenic conditions along major, secondary and primary roads. Scenic roadways have roadside corridors of special aesthetic, cultural or historical value. The corridor may contain outstanding scenic vistas, unusual geologic or other elements, all providing enjoyment for the traveler.

BACK COUNTRY ACCESS

These include corridors along back country roads which have scenic, historical, archaeological or other public interest values. This access may vary from a single track bike trail to a low speed paved road that traverses back country areas.

WILD RIVERS

Wild river areas are those rivers or sections of rivers that are free of impoundments and generally inaccessible except by trail, with watersheds or shorelines essentially primitive and waters unpolluted. These represent vestiges of primitive America. Wild means undeveloped; roads, dams or diversion works are generally absent from a quarter mile corridor on both sides of the river.

SCENIC RIVERS

Scenic river areas are those rivers or sections of rivers that are generally free of impoundments with shorelines or watersheds still largely primitive and shorelines largely undeveloped but accessible in places by roads. Scenic does not necessarily mean the river corridor has to have scenery as an outstandingly remarkable value; however, it means the river segment may contain more development (except for major dams or diversion works) than a wild segment and less development than a recreational segment. For example, roads may cross the river in places but generally do not run parallel to it.

RECREATIONAL RIVER AREAS

Recreational river areas are those rivers or sections of rivers that are readily accessible by road or railroad that may have some development along their shorelines and that may have undergone some impoundment or diversion in the past.

I.   RECREATION ACTIVITIES/USES ASSOCIATED WITH THESE RECREATIONAL AREAS

- ■ Camping
- ■ Fishing
- ■ Trapping
- ■ Hunting
- ■ Boating
- ■ Hiking
- ■ Backpacking
- ■ Horseback
- ■ Water Sports (Rivers, Lakes, etc.)
- ■ Recreational Gold Panning
- ■ Off Highway Vehicle - Motorized
- ■ Off Highway Vehicle - Non-Motorized (Mountain Bikes, etc.)
- ■ Hang Gliding (Aerial Activities)
- ■ Rock Climbing
- ☐ Resorts
- ■ Hobby Collecting (Rock Hounding)
- ■ Cultural Activities
- ■ Caving
- ■ Party Areas
- ■ Special Events
- ■ Educational Programs

II. POTENTIAL IGNITION RISKS IN THESE RECREATIONAL AREAS

- ☐ Wildland/Urban Interface
- ☐ Wildland/Urban Intermix
- ■ Maintenance Projects
- ☐ Construction Projects
- ☐ Power Lines/Substations
- ☐ Agriculture/Ranching
- ■ Mining
- ☐ Railroads
- ■ Power Equipment
- ■ Water Based Recreation
- ■ Campgrounds
- ■ Transportation Corridors
- ■ Fireworks
- ■ Shooting Areas
- ■ Children with Matches
- ■ Incendiary
- ☐ Debris Burn
- ☐ Slash Burn
- ☐ Timber Operations
- ■ OHV
- ■ Hunters
- ■ Fishermen
- ■ Party Areas
- ■ Trails/Hikers
- ■ Camps/Resorts
- ■ Business

- ■ Schools
- ☐ Dumps
- ■ Dispersed Recreation
- ■ Fuelwood/Equipment
- ☐ Communication Sites
- ■ Cultural Activities
- ☐ Drug Labs/Cultivation

III. POTENTIAL FIRE CAUSES IN THESE RECREATIONAL AREAS

- ■ Cooking/Warming Fire
- ■ Smoking
- ☐ Trash Burning
- ☐ Burning Vehicle
- ■ Exhaust/Catalytic Converter
- ☐ Logging Line
- ☐ Brakeshoe
- ☐ Burning Dump
- ☐ Field Burning
- ☐ Land Cleaning
- ☐ Slash Burning
- ☐ Right-of-Way/Ditch Burning
- ☐ Resource Management Burn
- ☐ Grudge Fires
- ■ Intentional (Arson, Employment, Pyromania, etc.)
- ☐ Blasting
- ☐ Burning Building
- ■ Playing with Matches

☐ House/Stove Spark

☐ Power Line/Transformer

■ Fireworks

☐ Welding

☐ Railroad

■ Shooting

Recreation Area Prevention Activities   *3.0*

Recreation areas generate, by their existence, a potential for increased ignition by concentrated public use. The fire prevention planning process should assess these different types of activities and design strategies to reduce ignitions and loss and damage from wildfires. Areas to consider can cover the following:

- Recreation Area Site Evaluations

- Signing

- Public Contacts

- Patrol

- Law Enforcement

- Enforcement—Permits

- Fire Safe Evaluations—Spark Arresters, Mufflers & Power Lines

Recreation Area Site Evaluations   *3.1*

I. RECREATION AREA FIRE SAFE EVALUATIONS

A planned site evaluation should be established for all public and private recreation facilities to determine if the operation is maintained in a fire safe manner. These evaluations should focus on hazard fuel conditions, fire safe structures and risk of ignitions by any area projects or operations.

A. Evaluations Scheduling

Every effort should be made to obtain compliance with fire safe practices and to develop good fire prevention attitudes and response from those contacted.

It is recommended that a minimum of three evaluations of each recreation area be made annually.

1. The first evaluation should be made during the early spring. The prime purpose of this contact will be to acquaint the owner/operator with recommended fire safe measures or to implement necessary fire prevention engineering actions on public facilities.

2. The second evaluation should be made early in the fire season.

3. The third evaluation should be made prior to mid fire season.

4. Further evaluations should be made until the area is in a fire safe condition.

5. During these evaluations, which should be made with the individual(s) responsible for the managing/maintaining recreation area, special attention should be given to mitigate hazardous conditions and fuels that exist.

B. Report of the Evaluation

A Report of Evaluation should be made out for each inspection and a notification of all hazards will be submitted to the fire manager and personnel responsible for the recreation program.

C. Corrective Action

Handle items that need corrective action immediately and provide expertise and assistance as needed.

Recommended corrective actions that are not implemented in a timely manner should be addressed until appropriate action is taken.

Signing

Signing is a technique used to convey wildfire prevention messages and provide visual information/education concerning a variety of wildfire prevention needs to general and specific public audiences. Fire managers should integrate signing into their fire management programs and identify specific signing and sign requirement needs in the prevention plan.

Carefully located signs in recreation areas with selected messages are effective tools in preventing damage and losses due to wildfire. Poor signing practices waste funds and can have an adverse effect on the prevention program. Prevention signing can be:

- Informational — Advising the public of ways to prevent fires (example: "Completely extinguish smoking materials.").

- Regulatory — Keeping audience informed of what they must do to prevent fires (example: "Campfires permitted only in developed camping areas.").

- Prohibitive — Emphatically stating what fires or acts are prohibited (example: "Fire restrictions currently in effect; campfire permits required.").

Examples of signing activities are:

- Replace posters to maintain a fresh look and correct message.

- Make necessary repairs to existing sign mountings (stain, straighten, etc.).

- Install new sign mountings as per approved sign plan.

- Compile data for sign plan update.

- Determine areas where new signs are needed.

I. PRINCIPLES AND GUIDELINES

A. Requirements

Fire prevention signs and posters must be designed, installed and maintained to achieve the important goals of effectively conveying a wildfire prevention message while portraying a positive agency image. To be effective, signs and posters should:

1. Convey the proper message(s) for the location. Make sure signs are up-to-date and appropriate.

2. Convey a clear, positive, friendly and simple message(s). Avoid areas full of "No" and "Do Not" messages and areas where there are too many signs/posters with conflicting messages, etc.

3. Command attention and generate respect for the agency and the environment. Never post signs on trees, fence posts, etc.

4. Display signs and posters on proper and well-maintained mounts. Keep sign and poster mountings in good condition and clear of vegetation and clutter. Promptly replace signs and posters that are worn or damaged.

B. Placement and Installation

Signs should be located with both the viewer and the message in mind. When selecting a site, consider whether the sign will be visible and readable for the viewer and strive to maximize each of these elements. Additionally, select locations which maximize the opportunity for the sign to convey its intended message. For example, a campfire message would be more appropriate and effective along a road leading to popular camping areas than it would be if located in an urban area.

C.	Placement

As a general rule, place signs on the right-hand side of the roadway as close to the roadway as authorized. Consider the following guidelines when selecting sign installation locations:

1.	Obtain necessary approvals from the appropriate right-of-way owner (city, county, state).

2.	Place signs where they provide adequate time for viewers to see and read the message, considering such things as approach speed, road conditions, etc.

3.	Select locations that minimize viewing obstructions. Some common placement locations to be avoided, if possible, include:

   a.	Dips in the roadway or trail.

   b.	Just beyond the crest of a hill.

   c.	Where the sign may interfere with the normal operation of a business or industry.

   d.	Too close to trees or other foliage that could cover the face of the sign.

4.	Place roadway signs within the driver's "cone of vision."

   a.	As speed increases, driver concentration increases, the focal point is more distant but also more narrowly defined.

   b.	As speed decreases, driver concentration wanes. At 25 mph the eye's natural focus point lies 600 feet ahead of the car. At 45 mph it lies 1,200 feet ahead.

c. As speed increases, the driver's peripheral vision decreases. On low-speed roads, the signs can be set further back from the right-of-way and still be seen and be effective. At 25 mph a driver's "cone of vision" is 90 degrees wide. At 45 mph it narrows to 65 degrees and at 60 mph is only 40 degrees wide.

d. As speed increases, a driver's ability to focus on foreground detail decreases. At 40 mph the closest point of clear vision lies 80 feet ahead of the car. At 60 mph the driver can see clearly only that detail within an area 1,000 to 1,400 feet in front of the car and within that 40 degree "cone of vision." At that speed, the car travels the distance between 110 feet and 1,400 feet in about 15 seconds.

5. Guidelines for the installation of signs along roadsides are as follows:

a. Height - The bottom of the sign should be a minimum of five feet above the level of the roadway.

b. Lateral Clearance - The distance from the edge of the roadway to the inner edge of the sign can range from six to twelve feet. The normal minimum is six feet. In cases where roadside topography precludes the six-foot minimum, the inner edge of the sign shall be no closer than two feet from the outer edge of a road's shoulder. Some right-of-way owners may require greater clearances.

c. Canting - Normally signs should be mounted approximately 93 degrees to the direction of, and facing, those they are intended to serve. This canting aids in reducing unwanted reflections which can be a safety hazard. Sign faces are normally vertical; but on grades, it may be desirable to tilt a sign three degrees back from the vertical to improve readability.

6. When choosing and maintaining a site for a sign, be aware of and avoid "sign clutter," a situation in which new and different signs are added to a location over time. This type of clutter creates an information overload and forces viewers to mentally wade through a mass of uncoordinated data to obtain the information they need. In the process, your fire prevention message can be overlooked and its effectiveness nullified.

    Try to locate fire prevention signs away from other government or private informational signs. Where this is not possible, or when other signs crowd an area over time, work with the other sign owners to evaluate the site and possibly combine, redesign or reduce the number of signs to avoid a cluttered appearance.

D. Sign Characteristics

In order to achieve optimum readability, sign and poster sizes will vary depending on the speed, if any, the viewer is expected to be traveling as he or she moves past the sign and the distance between the sign and the viewer. Adjusting the size of the lettering is the most common method of achieving readability.

E. Lettering Sizes

1. Moving Vehicles (according to estimated speeds)

More than 40 mph	6" letters
30 to 40 mph	5" letters
20 to 30 mph	4" letters
Less than 20 mph	3" letters

2. Motorized Trails

More than 25 mph	3" letters
Less than 25 mph	2" letters

3. Stationary Position - Non-Motorized Trail: 1-inch letters are adequate for most non-motorized trail situations.

4. Stationary Position - Interpretive/Informational Signs: Letter size for such signs is dependent upon the distance from which the message is to be viewed:

From 4 feet or less	5/8" letters
From 5 to 7 feet	3/4" letters
From 8 to 12 feet	1" letters
From 13 to 20 feet	2" letters
From over 20 feet	3" letters

F. Symbols

Symbol size also is a function of the viewing distance and the amount of time available for viewing. Use the following minimum symbol sizes for the type of use indicated:

1. Roads

0 - 25 mph	12"
26 - 50 mph	18"
Over 50 mph	24"

2. Motorized Trails

0 - 25 mph	12"
Over 25 mph	18"

3. Non-Motorized Trails

Viewed from 0 - 20 feet	3 - 4 "
Viewed from 21 - 75 feet	6"
Viewed from over 75 feet	8"

4. Waterways

Viewed from 0 - 150 feet	12"
Viewed from over 150 feet	18"

G. Maintenance

Signs should be maintained to ensure they can be easily read in both day and night hours. Replace or repair signs that have been defaced or when the lettering has been marred. Remove or cover signs when they are no longer needed or when the message is no longer applicable and timely. For instance, wildfire prevention signs left out during winter portray a disorganized agency and careless image. The effect of these messages are lost and agency image is publicly eroded.

In addition to maintaining the appearance and readability of the sign itself, remove weeds, brush, and other obstacles that obstruct the visibility of the sign or detract from the message and a positive agency image.

H. Sign Content

In determining the content for signs or posters, answer the following questions:

1. What is the purpose of the sign or poster? What problem does it address? Is the message appropriate?

2. Who is the intended audience?

3.   What do we want that audience to do, feel, think, or know after seeing the sign?

4.   What traits of the audience should be considered in choosing a sign?

5.   What is the message to be given to the target audience?

6.   Is a sign the appropriate media to use to deliver **that** message to **that** audience at **that** time and place?

7.   Are the message and design simple?

I.   Sign Mounts

Signs should be individually erected on separate posts or mountings, except where one sign supplements another or where route markers and directional signs must be grouped. Signs should be located so they do not obscure each other or are hidden by other objects.

Posts are used to hold signs in a permanent position and to resist swaying in the wind. Generally wood or metal posts are used. In areas where sign supports cannot be sufficiently offset from the road edge, use a suitable breakaway or yielding design. Concrete bases for sign posts should be flush with the ground level.

Metal posts should be unpainted galvanized metal. All hardware to affix the signs to either wood or metal posts should be either aluminum or galvanized.

After a sign installation is complete, the ends of the bolts should be snipped off and the threads disfigured or fractured to prevent removal of the nut by vandals or thieves.

The number and size of posts per sign should be proportional to the size of the sign. Generally, for signs up to 36 inches across use one post. For signs from 37 inches to 72 inches use two posts. For signs from 72 inches to 96 inches across use three posts.

II. POSTERS

A. Introduction

Posters are seasonal notices. They are normally constructed of short-lived material such as cardboard—many are plastic. They range in size from 11" x 9" items for use on camping or recreation area bulletin boards to large 54" to 44" highway posters.

B. Use

Posters are ideal ways of getting important messages to the target audience quickly. In most cases they are mounted on pre-existing poster or bulletin boards. Little more is needed than the poster and a staple gun. It is important that outdated posters be promptly removed.

Use the largest posters (54" x 44") only on high-speed highways (55 mph) and in situations where the scale of the country dwarfs their effect. Use these posters sparingly and place them far enough apart so that they do not appear to be repetitious.

Use medium-sized posters (42" x 34") on roads with speeds of 40-50 mph. Limit the use of these posters to essential locations.

The other medium-sized poster (44" x 16") is to be used on most low-speed, low-volume roads. To extend the use of fire poster mounts for sizes 42" x 34" and 44" x 16" through the off-fire season, other poster messages are available.

The smaller posters, such as 14" x 12" and 11" x 9", are designed for pedestrian traffic and for trails, campgrounds, trail heads, bulletin boards, roadside rests, and so on. The largest of these generally has adequate visibility and small message content and is suitable for low-speed, low-volume roads where such messages are needed; for example, "No Campfires."

Public Contacts   *3.3*

Agency personnel should communicate with as many recreation area users as possible. One-on-one contact to inform people of the need to be fire safe while using the wildlands is one of the most effective means of wildfire prevention. Contacts could include:

- Individuals, campers, hikers, hunters, etc.

- Groups - Boy/Girl Scouts, church camp, etc.

- Resorts, Camps

- Permittees

I. INDIVIDUALS

Individual public contacts by agency personnel are an important part of any fire program. To be effective you must carefully prepare for each contact you will make. The individual contact, delivered with enthusiasm "sells" the person on the safe use of fire and on the prevention of wildfire.

Examples of individual contacts you may be involved with include:

A. Campers at dispersed recreation areas

B. Campers at developed recreation sites

C. Water based recreation users (streams, lakes)

D. Off-highway vehicle users

E. Hunters, anglers

F. Hikers

G. Transient users traveling throughout an area

H. Local permittees

I. Woodcutters

II. GROUPS

While in recreation areas, opportunities may arise to provide wildland fire information to different groups.

Group contacts can be an effective way to increase awareness of fire prevention. The best results from group contacts are obtained when you tailor your program to meet the groups' interests or needs. Group contacts might include:

A. Homeowner associations

B. Camping groups (trailer, motorhome)

C. Equestrian associations

D. Outdoor/recreation associations

E. Boy/Girl Scout groups

F. Off highway vehicle groups

G. Ethnic groups

H. Outfitters/guides

I. Hiking groups

Patrol 3.4

There are many types of patrol activities appropriate to recreation areas. The following describes the most common types of patrol that can be utilized in recreation areas. However, there are others (canine, bicycle, etc.) that may also be effective. The Patrol Plan should identify which type of patrol is most efficient for an area. (For more detailed information on patrolling, refer to the "Wildfire Prevention Patrol Guide" June 1998, NFES #2570.)

- Ground Patrol (motorized) - The most common type of patrol. Highly effective in wildland urban interface areas and areas of concentrated public use.

- Foot Patrol - A patrol method for inaccessible areas and/or making one-on-one contacts.

- Aerial Patrol - An effective method of patrolling large areas in a short period of time.

- Mounted Horse Patrol - An effective method of trail, back country or off-road patrol.

- Motorcycle & All Terrain Vehicle Patrol - An effective method of trail or off-road patrol, especially in areas of off-road vehicle use.

I. GROUND PATROL (MOTORIZED)

A. The effectiveness of a ground patrol cannot be denied. The patrols can accomplish these basic missions:

1. Reduce the violation of fire laws.

2. Actively enforce fire and agency laws and regulations.

3. Provide information and assistance to area users and residents.

4. Provide quick initial attack on fires.

B. Ground patrols provide mobility and flexibility of operations. Wider coverage is, therefore, possible and considerably more tasks can be accomplished.

C. Ground patrols can be accomplished by a variety of personnel, patrol officers, volunteers, engine crews, other agency personnel, etc.

II. FOOT PATROL

Foot patrols can be a highly effective patrol method, especially in remote areas where other access is limited or not practical. This type of patrol places the agency personnel in direct contact with the public and provides a source of communication not otherwise readily available. Areas where foot patrol can be effective are:

A. Wilderness or back country areas

B. High-use recreation areas

C. Along rivers, streams, canyons, etc.

D. Trail systems

E. Dispersed campsites

F. Parks

G.   Special events

III.   AERIAL PATROL

Helicopters and fixed-wing aircraft can be used effectively for patrol. Aerial observation can provide:

A.   Locations of use (risk)

B.   Directions for maneuvering ground units to specific locations

C.   Detection of fires

D.   Patrol of large areas in a short period of time (dispersed recreation areas)

E.   Assistance in search and rescue

F.   Quick response

G.   Perspectives unavailable to ground units

H.   Dual purpose use, can be utilized with other resource and fire activities

IV.   MOUNTED HORSE PATROL

Mounted horse patrols once were the backbone of reaching and managing the wildlands. It is one of the oldest types of patrol. Today, mounted horse patrols are in limited use throughout the country. Areas with difficult access are conducive to mounted horse patrol. Patrolling large parks or areas on foot is obviously impractical, and in vehicles it is difficult to travel on surfaces other than paved. The horse can move effectively from one point to another, thereby reducing travel time and increasing efficiency. Mounted horse patrol can be highly effective in the following areas:

A.   Trails

B.   Wilderness and back country areas

C.   Parks

D.   Dispersed recreation areas

E.   High visibility events, planned and unplanned (parades, demonstrations, etc.)

V.   MOTORCYCLE AND ALL TERRAIN VEHICLE PATROL

Motorcycle and all terrain vehicle patrol is probably the least-used patrol method in wildland areas. However, it is an option that should not be eliminated from consideration. This method has proved effective in areas, such as:

A.   Off highway vehicle areas (roads/trails)

B.   Dispersed recreation areas

C.   Back country road systems

VI.   PATROL ACTIVITIES

Numerous activities can be accomplished while patrolling. These activities may include, but are not limited to:

A.   Informational Contacts

   1.   Individuals

   2.   Groups

   3.   Priority Contacts

B.   Signing — Installation and Maintenance

C.   Enforcement

    1.   Observe Inappropriate Conduct or Behavior

    2.   Complete Fire Investigations

    3.   Issue Permits and Contracts

    4.   Contract Fire Plans

    5.   Identify Restrictions and Closures

D.   Fire Safe Evaluations

    1.   Inspect Structures and Improvements

    2.   Observe Industrial Operations and Equipment Use (Agency & Private)

    3.   Check Spark Arresters, Mufflers and Power Lines

E.   Identify Hazard Fuel Reduction Locations

F.   Complete Patrol Documentation

*L*aw Enforcement

3.5

Law enforcement is used to gain compliance with fire ordinances and regulations and has secondary educational benefits. It is based on federal and state laws, agency regulations and local fire ordinances.

These laws are intended to regulate human activities and protect individuals using public lands and to protect natural resources from negligent or illegal acts that may result in a wildfire. When violations of these fire regulations are innocent and without major consequences, they may be handled administratively by issuing a written or verbal warning, or by some other response. Serious violations with major consequences may prompt more severe legal action such as citations, fines, etc.

I.   CONDUCT

Employees engaged in enforcement activities should display professionalism at all times. The following are a few professional characteristics of personnel with law enforcement responsibilities:

A.   Be courteous and helpful at all times, even during an emergency or incident.

B.   Have a desire to render a public service.

C.   Be able to explain the reasons for laws, regulations and the agency land management responsibility.

D.   Maintain the ability to recognize and avoid dangerous situations.

E.   Be aware of your authority to enforce the law, but always enlist the help of your agency or local law enforcement officer when approaching potentially dangerous situations or violators.

F.   Be familiar with the appropriate fire laws, statutes, ordinances, regulations and policies that apply to your agency.

Enforcement—Permits   3.6

The issuing of permits provides a one-on-one opportunity to discuss fire conditions, restrictions, etc., with the user. Making use of these opportunities with meaningful discussion of fire situations is more effective than merely passing out permits when they are required.

To be effective, permits must also be available as needed. Few things are as frustrating to a recreational visitor as arriving to find that permits are required but no one is available to issue them!

I.   CAMPFIRE PERMITS

Issuing campfire permits is an effective means of making personal fire educational contacts prior to the public's use of campfires. The permit specifies the elements of when, where and how the public may have cooking or warming fires.

There is a wide variance in the use of, or requirement for, campfire permits. Local fire prevention specialists can provide specific policies and procedures concerning campfire permits.

II. BURNING PERMITS

Burning permits are usually issued through a state authority and through the use of state documents and procedures. Requirements vary by state, so become familiar with the system for the local area.

Burning permits offer the following advantages:

A.   They provide documentation of the when, where, who and why of permits.

B. Prevention personnel have the option of issuing or not issuing permits according to fire conditions, timing, risks, etc.

C. Mitigation measures can be made part of the permit to reduce the potential for a burn to escape and become an uncontrolled wildfire.

D. Information about where and when burning will be done reduces costly false alarms.

E. Establish criteria that identify those conditions in which permits will not be used.

III. EXAMPLES OF PERMIT ACTIVITY WHILE ON PATROL:

A. Inspect permit sites.

B. Issue necessary permits.

C. Public contact with users in areas where permits are required.

*F*ire Safe Evaluations—*Spark Arresters & Mufflers*

3.7

I.   SPARK ARRESTERS & MUFFLERS

Mechanical equipment must comply with certain fire prevention regulations designed to reduce or eliminate the risk of fire. The high number of fire starts caused by equipment indicates these inspections are necessary and should receive high priority.

All gasoline, steam powered and diesel equipment used on recreational areas must be equipped with approved spark arresters or mufflers in working order.

Some examples of equipment requiring approved spark arresters or mufflers include:

- Construction, logging and mining equipment

- Vehicles (cars and trucks), motorcycles, ATVs

- Chainsaws

- Generators

- Locomotives

A current list of approved spark arresters for general purpose, locomotive and multiposition small engines can be found in the Spark Arrester Guide (PMS 430-2).

Examples of spark arrester/muffler activities while on patrol:

- On-site vehicle inspections.

- On-site stationary equipment inspections.

- Public contract with off highway vehicle users/groups.

- Provide inspection checks for the public, i.e., woodcutters.

*R*ecreation Area Fire Safe Practices *4.0*

The mitigation of potential ignitions in recreation areas can be effective by conducting and implementing the following fire safe practices:

- Fires and Fire Devices

- Evaluating Site Condition

- Treating Special Problem Areas

- Reducing the Recreation Area Fuels Hazard

Fires & Fire Devices *4.1*

I.   FIRES AND FIRE DEVICES

A.   Open Fires

This type of campfire is the most hazardous and should receive high priority.

1.   Campfires of this type are dangerous and should be confined to specific locations or designed fire pits.

2.   Proper clearance of flammable materials. The exact clearance will depend on circumstances at the scene. In no case should this clearance be less than 10 feet from the edge of the fire.

3.   Overhead clearance is important because of rising heat and sparks. There should be overhead clearance from combustibles of at least 20 feet.

4.   Steel or concrete campfire pits should be built and maintained by the owner/operator to encourage campers to build their fires in safe locations.

5.   The size of the fire pit should be regulated to allow only a small fire.

6.   If this type of campfire is left unattended, it can be extremely dangerous. The owner/operator should be encouraged to check camp site for unattended fires or a regular schedule.

B. Stoves

All camp stoves used in recreation areas should be checked to determine that they are maintained or used in a fire safe condition. Consider:

1. Proper clearance of flammable materials. The exact distance will depend on the conditions at the scene; however, in no case should clearance of flammable material be less than five feet from the stove. The same goes for overhead clearance.

2. The stove should be in good condition. It should not have holes in the fire box where coals or sparks could escape.

3. If the stove has a chimney, there should be a screen with holes no larger than $1/4$" over the outlet.

4. It is a common practice for campers to leave hot coals in a stove upon departing from an area. Therefore, camp stoves should be inspected with this thought in mind and recommendations for proper doors, etc., should be made.

5. Cleaning the camp stove.

    a. Make sure ashes are cool before handling.

    b. Shovel excess ashes from the pit into a non-combustible container that does not contain burnable garbage. Make sure all charred logs are inside the fire ring or stacked neatly beside it for use.

C. Barbecue Devices

Barbecue devices should be considered the same as campfires.

1. Proper clearance of flammable materials. The necessary clearance will depend on the circumstances at the scene. In no case should the clearance be less than 10 feet from the barbecue device.

2. Overhead clearance is not as critical when charcoal is being used in the barbecue device. However, if wood is being used to form coals for the barbecue, then clearance should be at least 20 feet overhead.

3. The disposal of coals before they are completely extinguished is a serious problem. Persons using barbecue devices should be warned to be absolutely sure the coals are extinguished before they are dumped out of the barbecue device.

D. Large Bonfires

Special precautions are necessary because of the fire size:

1. Flammable materials should be removed for a sufficient distance to make the fire safe. In no case should the clearing be less than 30 feet from the fire.

2. It is necessary that this type fire be located in an open area with no overhanging material.

3. The ground around the fire area should be free of all obstructions to eliminate the possibility of a person tripping and falling into the fire.

4. Recommend construction and maintenance of a circle of rocks around the fire area to confine the fire to a definite location.

Site Considerations

I. SITE CONDITIONS

A. Camp Sites

The use of a camp site can create fire problems. The inspection should consider general fire safe measures for the camp.

1. The camp site should be cleared of flammable material. The amount of clearing will depend on the size of the camp. It will normally be the area receiving the most use.

2. Dead and dying limbs should be removed from trees and brush for a height of 10 feet from the ground.

3. Areas used for camping overflow during periods of maximum use should meet all of the above requirements or be posted prohibiting campfires of any type.

4. Encourage locations of new camp sites in areas that are protected or partially protected from the wind.

B. Camp Parking Areas

Definite parking areas for each camp site should be developed. Campers should be required to park in these areas.

1. Dry grass or other flammable vegetation should be removed or cut to such a level that it cannot come into contact with the exhaust of vehicles parked in the area.

2. The entrance and exit should be so located that vehicles will not have to maneuver in such a manner that exhaust systems will come into contact with flammable material.

C. Perimeter Firebreaks

The location of the firebreaks will depend on the size of the facility and the location of the individual camp sites. It might be practical to construct a firebreak around groups of camp sites, or it might be better to construct a firebreak around the entire facility. Terrain, fuels and effectiveness should dictate proper procedures. The value of the perimeter firebreak should be explained to the responsible party. Stress restricting the spread of a fire that might start on-site as well as the fact that an approaching fire might be kept from reaching the recreation area.

1. The firebreak should be clear of all flammable material. The width will depend on the terrain and fuels in the area; however, the minimum width should be 10 feet.

2. A 25 foot wide fuel break, containing a five foot firebreak, may be recommended instead of the 10 foot firebreak.

3. The firebreak, to be effective, must be continuous.

D. Access Roads

1. Access roads and all roads within the recreation area should be fireproofed.

2. Encourage maintenance of two access roads for the recreation area. This will greatly reduce the possibility of campers being "trapped" in case of fires and will also allow campers to leave while fire equipment is responding to the area.

3.   A road around the perimeter of the recreation areas also serves very well as fuel and firebreak.

E.   Refuse Disposal

The disposal of refuse from campgrounds can be a major problem. The Inspecting Officer should advise of the legal requirements and other fire prevention measures pertaining to dumps.

F.   Equipment

Most recreational areas will have some type of mechanical equipment on the premises. This will include such items as light plants, pump motors, bulldozers, or chain saws.

Fire prevention inspections should include the fire safe operation of all equipment on site.

G.   Safety Islands

If the campground is located in an area of hazardous fuels and access roads are limited, encourage establishment of "fire safety" zones. Publish and post evacuation routes to these areas in the event of a fire.

Special Problem Areas   4.3

I.   SPECIAL PROBLEM AREAS

In addition to the fire risks and hazards mentioned, inspections will find problems that are unique to the specific recreation facility.

A.   Undeveloped Camp Areas

1.   These are usually areas without facilities that are used for camping purposes. Because of this use, they have become camping areas, without the improvements of developed camping sites.

a.   These unimproved campground areas are usually found along rivers, streams or small lakes and canyon bottoms.

b.   Inspections will be guided in these areas by local policy and the fire and recreation program manager.

c.   If they are unauthorized, then the inspector should follow agency procedures regarding illegal camp areas.

2.   If these types of campgrounds are allowed, inspections should consider the following items:

a.   Proper permits (camping, campfires, etc.) should be checked for possession and compliance.

b.   Campfires should only be allowed in safe locations. If the location of the fire is not safe, then the inspector should request that the fire be put out and re-established in a safe location.

  c. Ten feet of clearance around the campfire should be the minimum. In most cases, the inspector should require more clearance because of the lack of any type of supervision of the area.

  d. Clearance around the camp site area will usually be handled by requiring all fires to be built in safe locations.

  e. When inspecting this type of camp site, the inspector should always obtain the name and address of a person at the location. License numbers of cars parked at the location should also be recorded.

  f. Plans should be made for intensive fire prevention patrol during times of high recreation use or high fire hazard.

B. Water Recreation Areas

There are several special problems connected with this type of recreation area.

  1. Of prime importance is the establishment of sufficient parking areas to handle all vehicles and boat trailers. Parking areas should be clearly established and free of all flammable fuel.

  2. All fuel storage buildings should have 30 feet clearance from flammable materials.

    a. "No Smoking" signs should be posted around fuel storage and dispensing areas.

b. Advise users about the policy concerning dispensing gasoline in glass or plastic containers. It is a very unsafe practice and regulations or local ordinances may make it illegal.

3. A critical fire hazard associated with these operations is the establishment of picnic and camp areas along the lake shore where the only access is by water. Patrol becomes exceedingly difficult; however, fire prevention measures should be far more strict than for a normal camp or picnic site. (Regulations of the agency controlling the use of water recreation areas should be carefully checked, as well as local governing agency ordinances or regulations, prior to taking the actions recommended below.)

a. The docking facility should be posted advising recreationists that picnicking and camping is allowed only at designated sites.

b. No open campfires should be allowed at the camp sites. Camp stoves or barbecue pits should be furnished instead.

c. There should be a minimum of 10 feet clearance around all camp stoves and barbecue pits.

d. All flammable material should be removed from the camp sites.

e. Groups of camp sites should be enclosed within a firebreak.

f. Camping areas should be posted with signs requiring all campfires to be confined to camp stoves, barbecue or fire pits.

g. The owner/operator should be encouraged to conduct periodic daily fire safe patrols of the area.

*R*educing the Recreation Area *Fuels Hazard*   *4.4*

Fuels are classified as live and dead combustible materials. Hazardous wildland fuel situations are where there are areas of flammable vegetation and where there is a combination of flammable fuel and moderate to steep topography. These hazardous situations can be found in remote areas as well as in areas where wildland vegetation is intermixed with structures.

Hazardous fuel situations can occur naturally or as a result of human activities. Areas of hazardous fuels produce severe fire behavior, contribute to disastrous wildfires, are resistant to fire suppression efforts, and create a great potential for property, life and resource loss.

Fuels management is the manipulation and reduction of hazardous fuels to meet fire management objectives. Fuels management is accomplished through a variety of fuel treatment strategies such as piling and burning timber slash; manipulating vegetation (greenstripping); fuel modification or removal along roadways and near structures and developments; prescribed fire projects; etc.

Fuel treatment projects properly implemented and maintained in specific areas can effectively reduce fire hazards. This is an effective application of wildfire prevention actions which can reduce the potential loss of natural resources and property while reducing agency fire suppression costs. Hazard reduction plans and projects should be outlined in the local fire management, fuels and fire prevention plan.

Examples of hazard reduction activities to be inspected while on patrol:

- Proper hazard reduction around dispersed recreation area campfire sites.

- Hazard reduction maintained in areas of concentrated public use: roadside turnouts, scenic areas, parking areas, etc.

- Developed recreation areas: fuel clearance around stoves, tables, toilets, etc.

- Completed fuel and firebreaks in hazardous fuel areas.

- Hazard reduction completed around all agency and private structures and improvements.

Recreation Area—Fire Safe Site Design Recommendation 5.0

The design of recreation areas is an important element in reducing loss by wildfire. Design considerations should consider:

- Recreation Road System

- Parking Locations

- Camping Area (cooking, eating)

- Hike-In Sites

Fire Safe Site Design Recommendation—
Recreation Road Systems

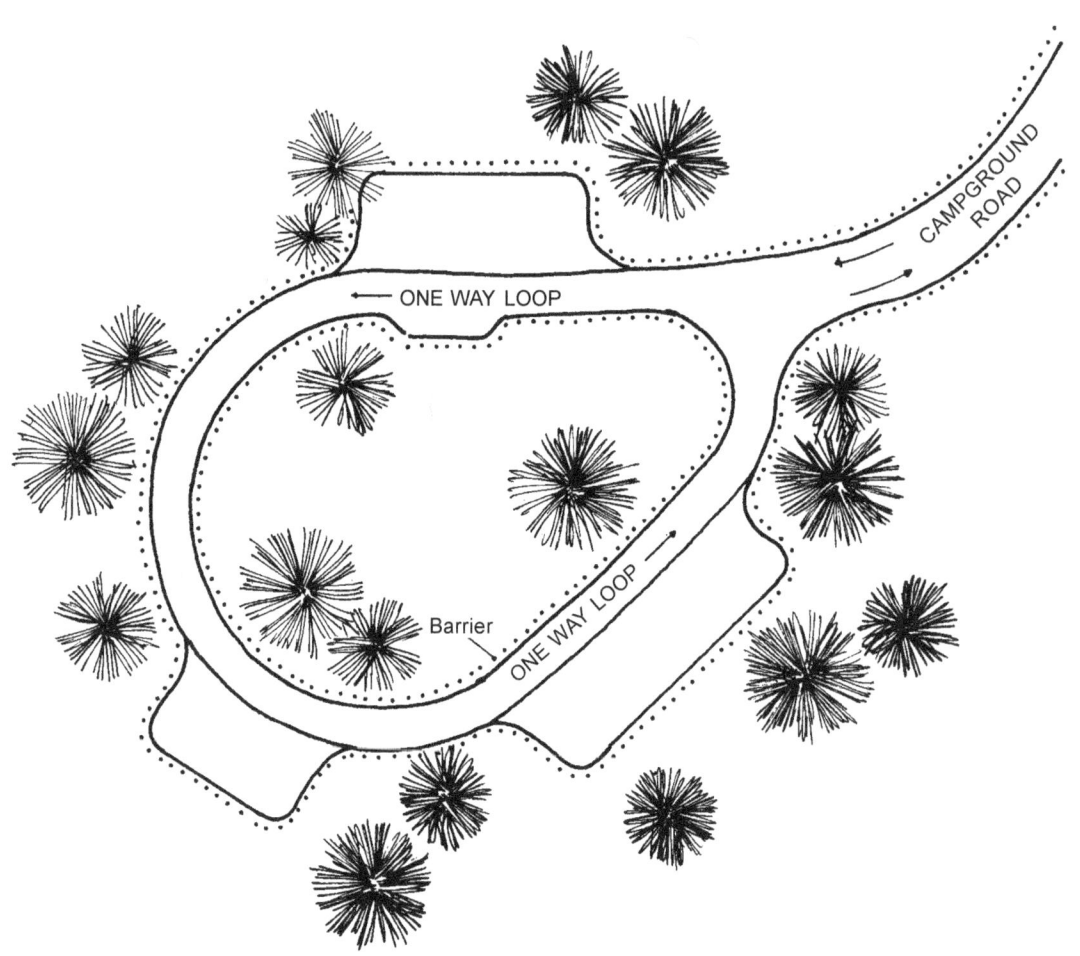

CAMPGROUND ROAD

ONE WAY LOOP

ONE WAY LOOP

Barrier

• • • • • Fuel Reduction Zone

*F*ire Safe Site Design Recommendation— *Camping Areas*

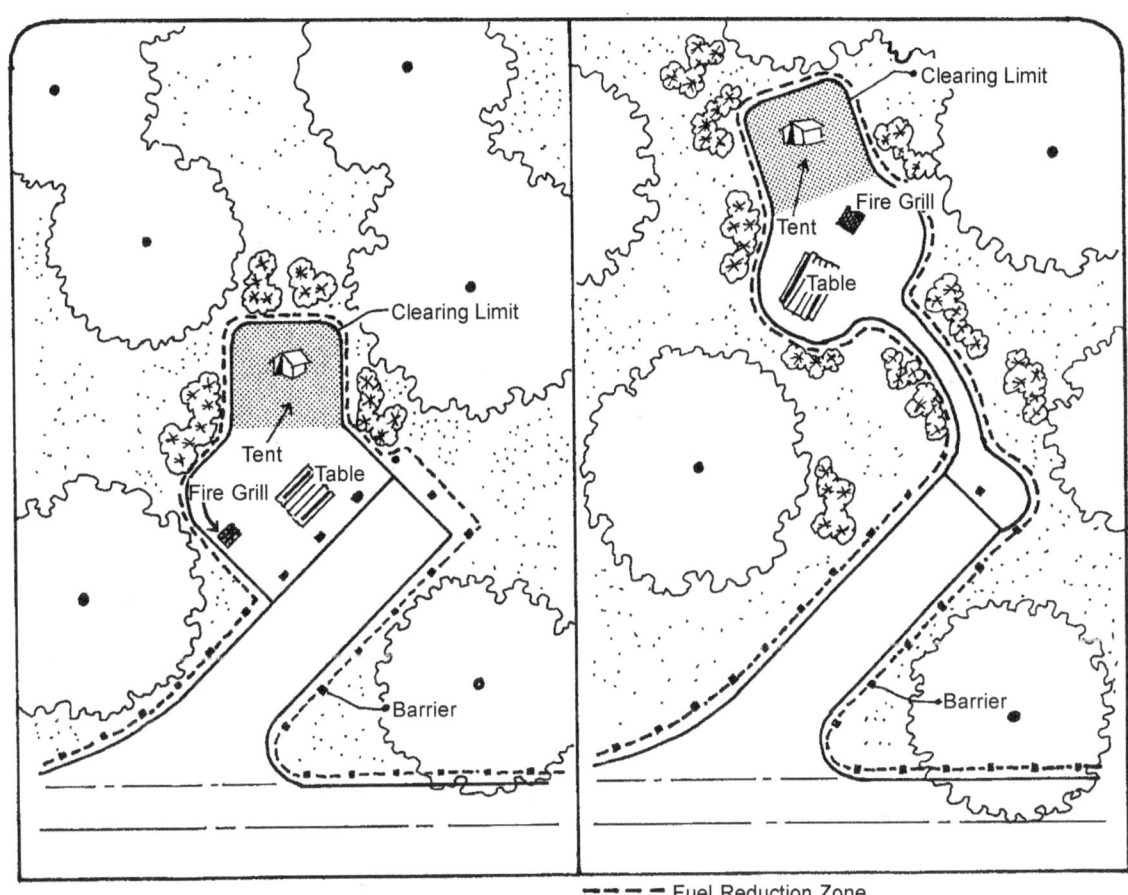

Clearing Limit

Tent

Fire Grill

Table

Barrier

Clearing Limit

Fire Grill

Tent

Table

Barrier

‑ ‑ ‑ ‑ Fuel Reduction Zone

*F*ire Safe Site Design Recommendation—
Walk-In Sites

5.3

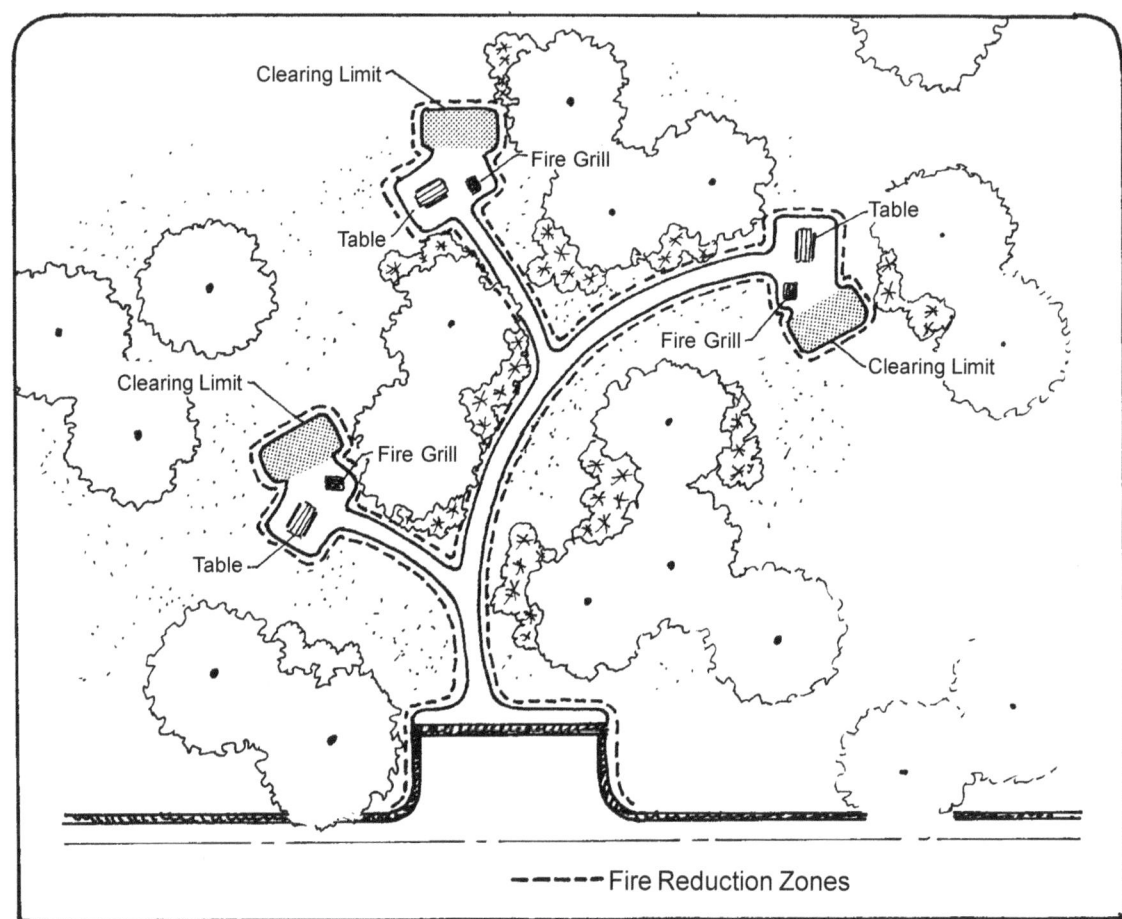

Appendix

RECREATION AREA
FIRE EVALUATION REPORT

Site Location _____

In the interest of fire safety, inspections of recreation areas are being conducted. The following checklist shows items that have been reviewed and makes recommendations for improvement. These changes will greatly increase the chances of protecting the property and the adjacent lands from loss or damage by wildfire.

I.	CAMP STOVES	Adequate	Inadequate	Remarks
A.	Maintained adequately			
B.	Ashes removed			
C.	Outlets cleaned			
D.	Fire box adequate			
E.	Concrete adequate			
F.	Metal free of defects			
G.	Fire ring adequate			

II.	VEGETATION CLEARANCE	Adequate	Inadequate	Remarks
A.	Camp stove			
B.	Disposal sites			
C.	Overhead clearance adequate			
D.	Camping area free of flammable vegetation			
E.	Is adequate flammable material removed?			

III.	ACCESS ROUTES/PARKING	Adequate	Inadequate	Remarks
A.	Roadside hazard reduction complete			
B.	Flammable vegetation removed from parking areas			

IV.	PUBLIC SAFETY	Adequate	Inadequate	Remarks
A.	Adequate egress/exit available			
B.	Fuelbreak system in place			
C.	Exterior road system adequate			
D.	Interior road system adequate			

V.	SITE LOCATION CONDITIONS	Adequate	Inadequate	Remarks
A.	Slope			
B.	Topography			
C.	Aspect			
D.	Natural barriers			
E.	Protected from wind			

RECREATION AREA
FIRE EVALUATION REPORT
(continued)

__RECOMMENDED CORRECTIVE ACTION(S)__ _____

_____

_____

_____

_____

_____

_____

_____

_____

Inspector _____   Agency _____

Date Evaluated _____   Phone _____

www.ingramcontent.com/pod-product-compliance
Lightning Source LLC
Chambersburg PA
CBHW081140290526
45795CB00006B/2308